by George Shannon

illustrated by
Jose Aruego
and Ariane Dewey

A Mulberry Paperback Book, New York

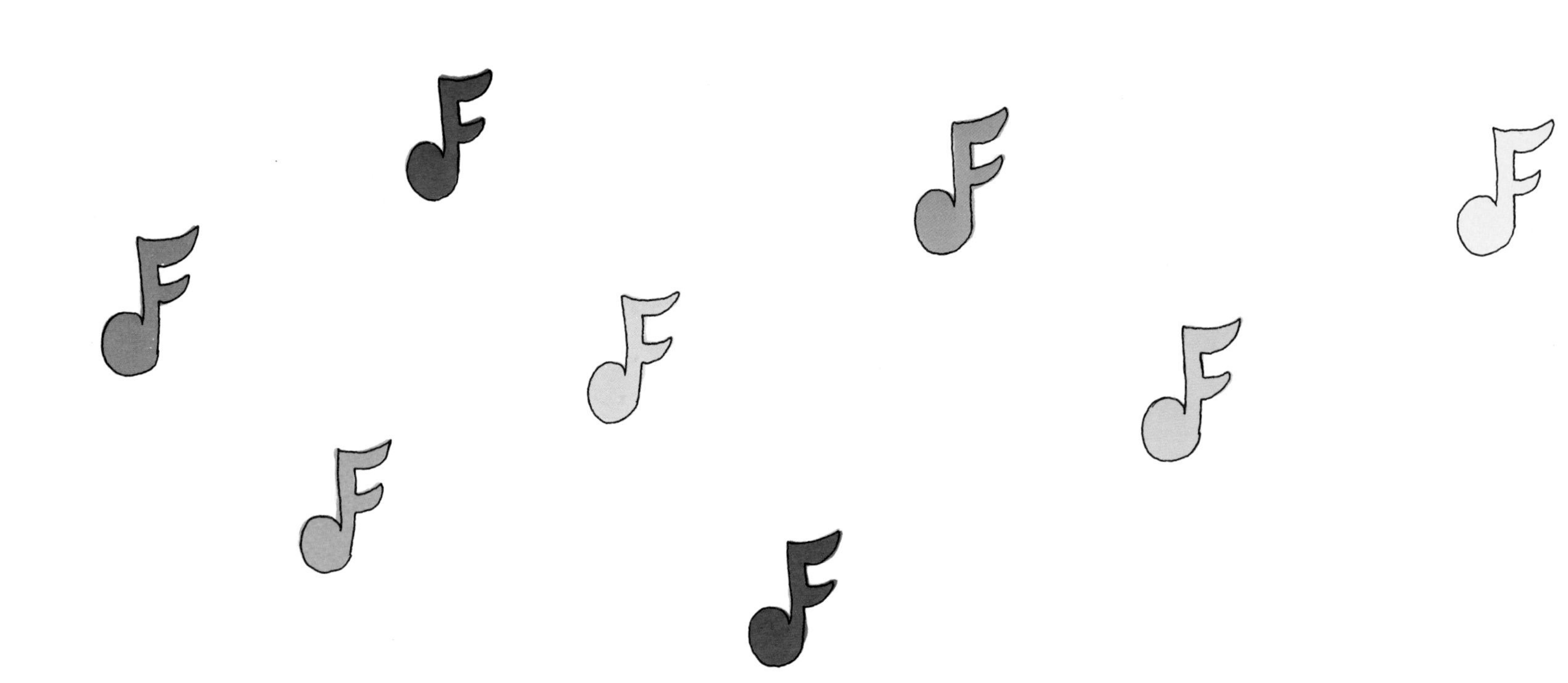

Printed in the United States of America
First Mulberry Edition, 1992.

10 9 8 7 6 5 4 3

Library of Congress
Cataloging in Publication Data
Shannon, George. Lizard's song.
Summary: Bear tries repeatedly to learn Lizard's song. [1. Bears—Fiction. 2. Lizards—Fiction]
I. Aruego, Jose. II. Dewey, Ariane. III. Title.
PZ7.S5287LF [E] 80-21432
ISBN 0-688-11516-0

TO DIANE WOLKSTEIN

–G.S.

TO JUAN

–J.A. and A.D.

Lizard lived in the mountains of the west.
He liked it there and lived on a big flat rock.
He was so happy living there
that he often made up songs.

They were not fancy songs, but they were his.
Almost every day he would dance about
on his rock singing a song:

"Zoli zoli zoli—zoli zoli zoli
Rock is my home—rock is my home
Zoli zoli zoli—zoli zoli zoli..."

One day Bear heard him singing. Bear was the kind who, when he saw something he liked, took it. Bear liked Lizard's song and he wanted it. He ran up to Lizard's rock and said, "Teach me that song. I want it!"

Lizard was glad to share his song. "Sit down," he said,
"I will sing it over and over until you know it.

Zoli zoli zoli–zoli zoli zoli
Rock is my home–rock is my home
Zoli zoli zoli."

He had to sing it ten times before Bear learned it.
"I know it now," said Bear and off he went
singing and dancing.

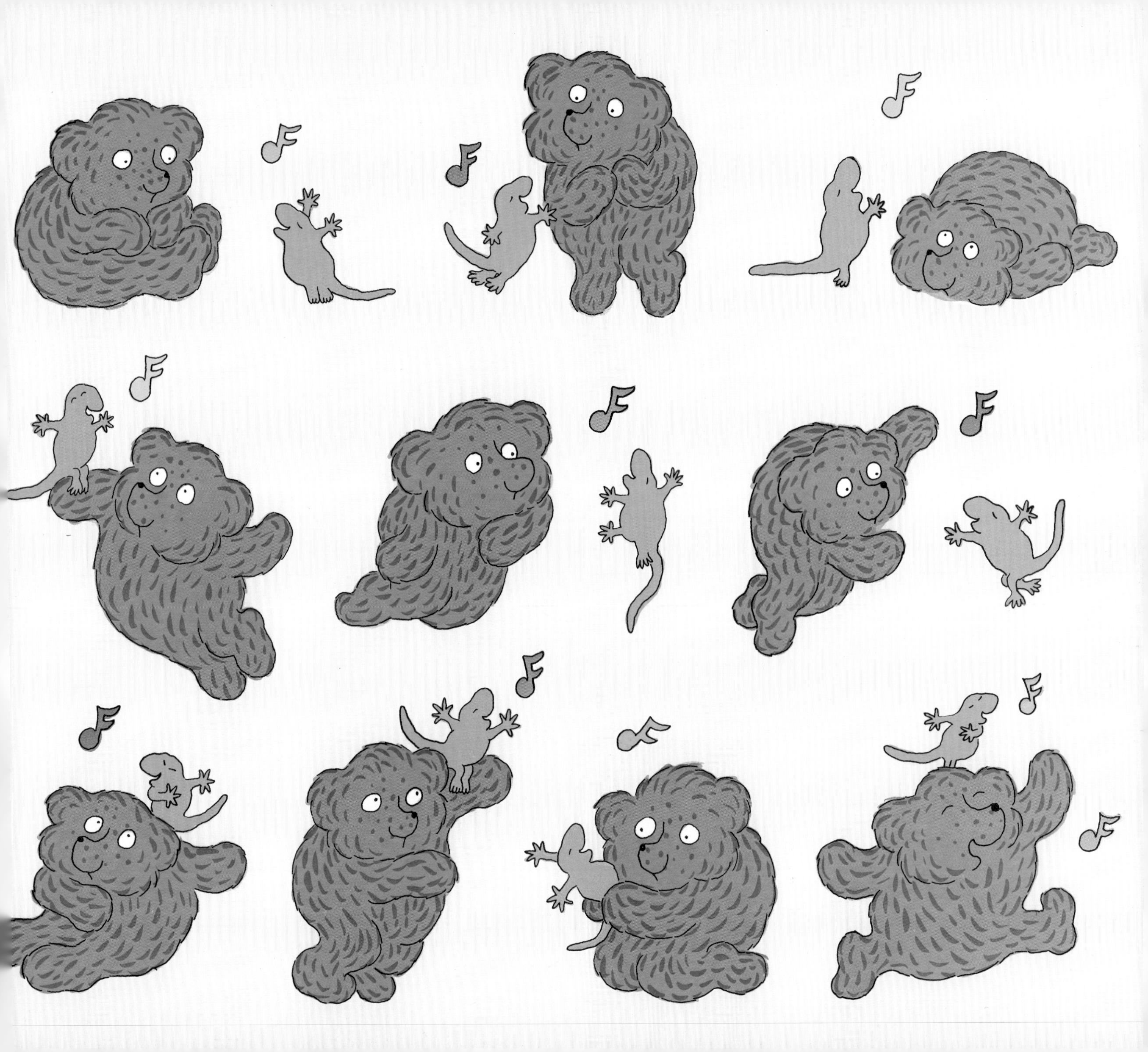

"Zoli zoli zoli – Rock is my home –

Zoli zoli zoli"

He was so busy singing he didn't see the pond. "QUACK QUACK QUACK QUACK!" The ducks on the pond heard Bear and flew off right past his nose. Bear was so startled he forgot the song.

QUACK
QUACK
QUACK
QUACK
QUACK
QUACK
QUACK

He ran back to Lizard's rock.
"Lizard, teach me the song again. I forgot."
Lizard sang the song over and over again.
"Zoli zoli zoli…"
After the twelfth time Bear said, "I know it."
And off he went.

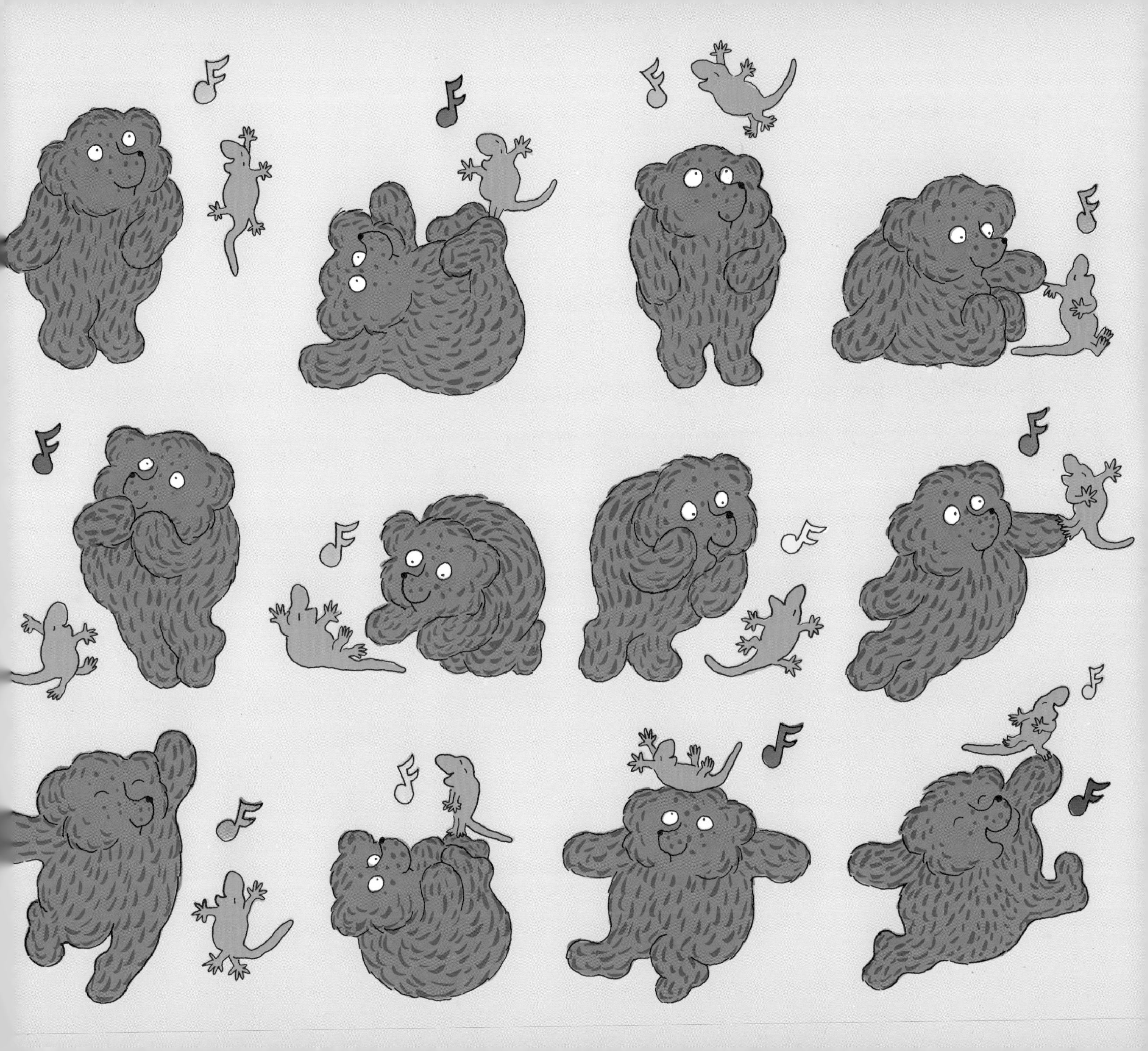

Bear was very proud of his song. He went singing and dancing across the land, "Zoli zoli zoli zoli zoli..."

SWISH! A rabbit jumped out of its hole and right past Bear. Bear chased after, but the rabbit was faster.

The rabbit got away and so did the song. Bear could not remember a single note, not even "Zo–"

He started back to Lizard's rock. "Lizard," said Bear,
"teach me that song." Bear asked time and time again.
But Lizard was asleep. He didn't hear a word.
Bear did not know what to do.
He thought, and then quickly scooped Lizard up in a sack.
He would take Lizard home with him, that's what he'd do.
He had Lizard in the sack, but it was a quiet trip home—
no song to sing, nor dances to do.

As he walked along, the sack swung about. Lizard woke up.
No sun, no moon. All he could see was dark.
Lizard was scared. He quietly began to sing his song.

"Zoli zoli zoli–zoli zoli zoli
Rock is my home–rock is my–"

Bear heard him.
He stopped and dropped the sack.
"Lizard, teach me your song. I want it."

"Bear," said Lizard, as he crawled out of the sack,
"my song is about rocks. My song is about me.
What about you, Bear? What is your home?"
"Den," answered Bear. "Den is my home."

Lizard thought, and smiled, then began to sing,
"Zoli zoli zoli–zoli zoli zoli
Rock is my home, what is your home?
Zoli zoli zoli."
Bear listened twice, then began to sing too.

"Zoli zoli zoli–zoli zoli zoli
Den is my home–den is my home
Zoli zoli zoli–zoli zoli zoli."

They sang and danced all the way home,
Lizard to his rock and Bear to his den.

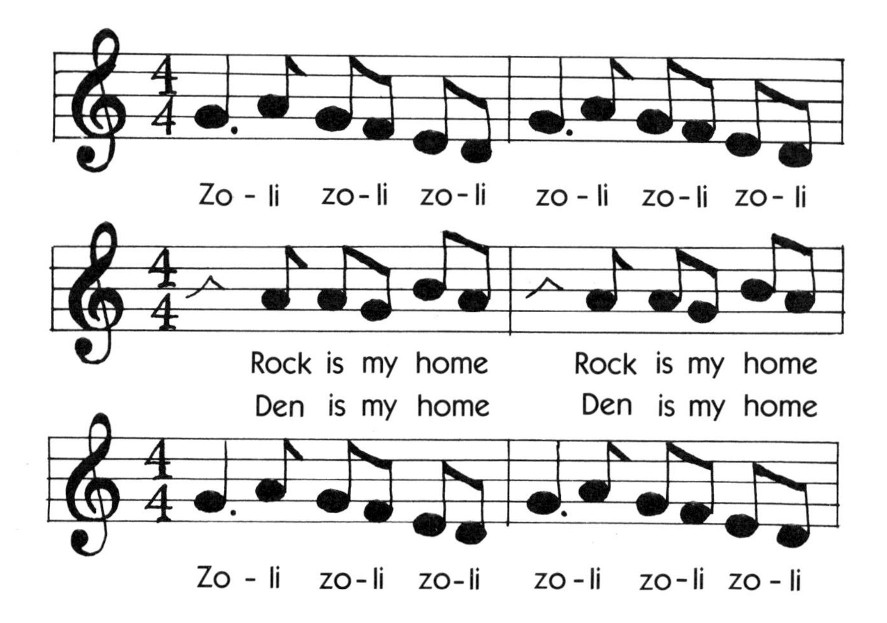

"Zoli zoli zoli–zoli zoli zoli
Den is my home–den is my home
Zoli zoli zoli–zoli zoli zoli."

"Zoli zoli zoli–zoli zoli zoli
Pond is my home–pond is my home
Zoli zoli zoli–zoli zoli zoli."

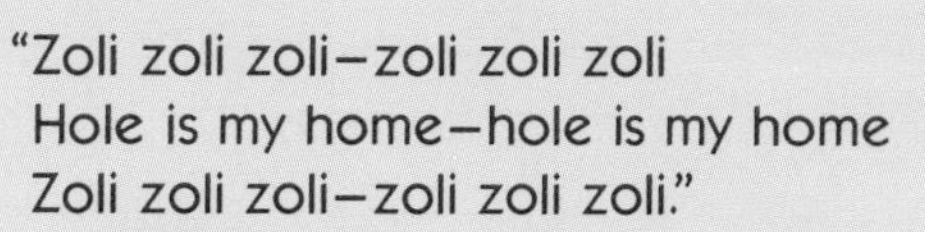

"Zoli zoli zoli–zoli zoli zoli
Hole is my home–hole is my home
Zoli zoli zoli–zoli zoli zoli."

"Zoli zoli zoli–zoli zoli zoli
Rock is my home–rock is my home
Zoli zoli zoli–zoli zoli zoli."